Jacci Bulman

In the holding

Indigo Dreams Publishing

First Edition: In the holding
First published in Great Britain in 2019 by:
Indigo Dreams Publishing
24, Forest Houses
Cookworthy Moor
Halwill
Beaworthy
Devon
EX21 5UU

www.indigodreams.co.uk

Jacci Bulman has asserted her/his right under the Copyright, Designs and Patents Act 1988 to be identified as the author of this work.
© Jacci Bulman 2019

ISBN 978-1-912876-14-3

British Library Cataloguing in Publication Data. A CIP record for this book can be obtained from the British Library.

This book is sold subject to the condition that it shall not, by way of trade or otherwise, be lent, re-sold, hired out, or otherwise circulated without the author's and publisher's prior consent in any form of binding or cover other than that in which it is published and without a similar condition including this condition being imposed on the subsequent purchaser.

Designed and typeset in Palatino Linotype by Indigo Dreams.
Cover design by Ronnie Goodyer at Indigo Dreams
Printed and bound in Great Britain by 4edge Ltd.

Papers used by Indigo Dreams are recyclable products made from wood grown in sustainable forests following the guidance of the Forest Stewardship Council.

for Brigid

'By the side of the everlasting Why there is a Yes —
a transitory Yes if you like, but a Yes'

~ E.M. Forster, 'A Room with a View'

Acknowledgements

With thanks to all who teach me poetry, especially the North Cumbria Stanza group, the Eden Poets, and Jan, Josephine and Dawn; to everyone who inspires my writing and teaches me love; to all the people involved in my book about faith, for teaching me to listen; to Nicki and my family; to my husband Alan, and to Kathleen, for her encouragement.

The poem *'Show me a day'* was runner up in the Mirehouse 'Words by the Water' 2018 poetry competition.

Also by Jacci Bulman:

A Whole Day Through From Waking, Cinnamon Press, 2016.
Write to be Counted: an anthology of poetry upholding human rights (Co-editor with Nicola Jackson and Kathleen Jones), The Book Mill, 2018.

CONTENTS

in the holding of the gift ...of love

Where only the river flowed 9
All there is 10
May Moon Spell 11
The Cock of The School and Wendy Brown 12
Two kids in the car on the long drive to the caravan 13
Two blue birds 14
How can our synchrony involve a sudden love 15
Chapel 16
Joan 17
A passion for 'Hurricane Higgins' 18
There are two kinds of weird 19
Sunk 20
A room in the city 21
Who's afraid? 22
Some things wanted 23
Scattered atoms 24
5-D 25
Solved 26

in the holding of the gift ...of communication

Shapes in clay 29
Lily 30
C. 31
Near Liboreiro 32
Oxford, night-swimming 33
Why Salmon Jump 34
No Translation 35
if 'red' were 'God' 36
the sound of quietness 37
Who can tell? 38

Some words are mine 39
Track through 40

in the holding of the gift ...of mortal, human life

Can we fail? 43
For Derek, who is blind 44
Phuc 45
At ease 46
Some vile tornado 47
18th Birthday at Bolton Street Working Men's Club 48
Tinfoil and curls 49
1st Choice 50
Uncovered 51
but by loving 52
Show me a day 53
Oneness 54
Clear 55
pondering on why did God make us? 56
Something good to think about 57
Jerusalem 58
It's not the same 59
Bravery 60
On the same street as the posh shoe-shops 61
Identity 62
Can Tell 63
Last winter 64
Laid flat on the mesh-metal bridge 65
Permanence 66
or in the arm-link of a friend 67
Purple 68
Jo and Bess 69

In the holding

in the holding of the gift ... of love

Where only the river flowed

Jo didn't know much, only that he needed to sleep.
Slept for a long time in a room smelling of
coconut and cheap perfume, and Bess didn't wake him. She left
the door ajar to be sure he stayed then let him lie there
      on her cream cotton sheets
while she sat drinking Tennessee in the kitchen through
the hours when even the soil is sleeping, and then again
when the sun was hot through the blinds.

She couldn't lie beside him, not knowing what he'd done,
how he'd got here, but,
      even though she knew it was wrong,
she got a kind of ease knowing he was there in her bed
sleeping deeper
than the well, and for a while she imagined
what they could have been, the two of them,
with a farm, chickens and a field full of barley, way out
nowhere, where the wood axe broke the quiet.

All there is

He says how she fell helping him move wood,
scraped her shins, cut her knee,
got the *zing* knocked out of her.

There's a clear regret in his voice –
that he wasn't able to protect her.

Sure, he knows of all the troubles going on
but right now, his intent is pure,
as if he's standing by a freezing lake and

all he can see is that one sweet coot in the lilies,
limping on icy pads.

May Moon Spell

If we lay ourselves down in a glade and refuse to go home
even when we really want our supper,
if we lie for hours surrounded by green beech leaves,
perfect with the bluebell blue,
and stay almost still, until we feel full of all we miss,
forget the fears in the house, pressures of the unfinished,
just lie as if invited so the creatures start to think
we belong, and nudge closer,
then we can fall asleep and the Old Lady of the Sky-Fair
will hand out long white ribbons
to thread through our dreams and weave us into the woods –
soak us with a light she does not own but is happy to share –
and all that we have buried will appear, in a room reached
by narrow ledges; with sharp drops which we shall leap across.

The Cock of The School and Wendy Brown

They sit on the red school wall,
gaze elsewhere:
everyone else looks up.

And when we play kiss-chase,
pin each other to the ground,
they hold their faces in the sun.

Two kids in the car on the long drive to the caravan

We would say it as if it were the entrance chant
to a world where the bond we felt
would persist forever.
Through the pile of *Snap!* cards,
past robin, seagull, peregrine...
until we came to the picture that allowed us,
for no reason known to ourselves,
to shout *KI-TTI-WAKE!*
and not even need to look at each other,
lifted by a sibling love that would,
in time, be buried under a volume of griefs,
but not forgotten.
I say it now to myself, *kittiwake*.

Two blue birds

tattooed on the woman's chest,
instead of breasts,

    yellow dashes,
    open wings.

Mum has two scars instead.
Dad's not seen them yet.
When I do,
I want to fold my arms.

Two blue birds, open wings,
carrying this woman and my mum,
who puts hers on with her bra,
like a pair of socks.

Heavy they are,
like balls of bread dough.
At home she is comfy just flat,
and I want to hold her.

How can our synchrony involve a sudden love of umbelliferous plants?

(for Nicki)

Even I am shocked when we call into a Whalley shop
and you immediately choose this post-card
of a fennel plant in black and white, because it looks like
gorgeous hog-weed
filling the verges you drive along,

while I can't stop taking photos right now
of water hemlock by the river,
with tiny red insects and bees
feeding on every flower-head.

Chapel

In a Welsh valley near Offa's Dyke,
inside those pastel coloured walls
like I saw sometimes in southern France,
lemon, pink, blue mottled with promises,
plaster cracked and fallen in places,
every wall at a skewed
angle to the next. No clear corner;
even the floor sloped.

There were no special decorations or
patterned windows, no cloths upon the altar.
We stood quiet, had no idea
years from now, we may both be looking
back on this visit as a time of hope,
a magic we believed would thread
right through our lives, hold them
unquestionably together.

Those walls were crooked
but true, and did we both leave a part of
ourselves there, in a capsule outside
this life, holding us in an unforeseen pause?

Joan

Clifford is telling us one of his stories
and we are laughing.
You, I see out the window
as you rush to pick us some spinach.

You come in with a bunch
of the biggest green leaves.
What about sweet peas...do you like sweet peas?
We nod and smile.

On goes your man with his yarn
as you return to the garden,
assured your husband is fair enjoying himself,
us being keen listeners.

Within minutes you're standing in the doorway,
hands full of pure white flowers which have
in their own way an intoxicating smell.
I want to tell you how beautiful they are

but there is only a short enough gap in
Clifford's tale – of your caravan days
on the Hebrides – for a quick
lovely and *thank-you*.

You join us.
Distracted now I watch your face
watching your man having a ball.
I sit quiet and you teach me kindness.

A passion for 'Hurricane Higgins'

     You give me a polka-dot beaker of Vimto
after school, progressing to tinned steak and Smash
when I'm home from college.
     Sometimes, if you're in the mood, you'll hold
the hem of your skirt in your hands and
do a little dance, or tell me of the nights
when you slipped out, heels in a bag,
coal-dust for eye-shadow, to go courting.
     You always push your chair right back
by the kitchen door – even though it blocks
my way through – so I push it forwards quick
when you get up but you sit down,
surreptitiously sliiiiiiiiiiide it back, whilst glued
to your snooker.

Until one day you tell me I've stolen your size 18
pleated tartan skirt – how I've always been a *little bloody thief.*
I implore you to believe this isn't true, until you apologise,
kind of, but are still convinced.
     Then suddenly you can't say your name or walk steady,
have to bang on your bedroom window for help –
within days put in a place with people holding their dresses
over their heads, crapping on the floor.
     When your face goes yellow, I know there isn't long,
take you cigarettes because now it doesn't matter.
You drop ash on your nightie, look up
and cannot speak.

But still you are, to me, beloved lady
with strangely webbed toes – like a cygnet, almost a swan,
your long arm waving, until I am out of sight.

There are two kinds of weird

One is like the night he was splitting with his wife and it was their last night together in the old tenement flat, so he was packing his things, making awkward moves, when a burglar's legs – the fool had somehow got in the attic – shot right through the kitchen ceiling, which meant they had to call the police and there he was, talking to the officer with that kind of weird feeling as in *this is wrong, there is something BAD about this I'm gonna regret for the rest of my life*, and the thief's legs dangle through the plaster while he tells the officer he was just packing and his guts say *weird* as in *bad weird, ugly weird this is. Shouldn't be.*

Then there's the other kind of weird, like with the woman he left his wife for, and they were heading for Heathrow to fly around the world when the blue Mercedes van they were driving around a busy London roundabout was held up by a team of ten police-men with machine guns all aimed at him as he stepped out of the van, which happened to be the same colour and type as the one just used by IRA terrorists, so he stood, being searched, with those rifles pointing at him, thinking *this is weird*, as in *surreal*, as in *I can't stop shaking*, which is kind of funny weird. Not like the first time.

Sunk

They are being served steaks in Brown's,
all around a big table for Rob's 21st.
He looks at her and she immediately dives in his eyes
like a Labrador chasing a stone thrown into a loch.

Then, just as her hot plate with heaps of potato mash
and onion rings arrives in front of her, he says it.
    She tries to pretend she hasn't heard,
        stupidly says *sorry, what?*
So, he says it again...*you're just like a sister to me...*

She looks at the unicorn pendant
dangling in her pile of peas,
like it's drowning in a green sea.

A room in the city

The young man whose house it is tried his best to shock
                    her after he had carried
all her suitcases, hoping she would stay long
                    enough to appreciate
the shape of him
   – a slight silhouette
in a pencilled work of art; but there are trumpets
                    in Trafalgar Square,
bright coloured hats at the market –
there are decades to skip along before she sees him
as a beautiful thing,
   missed.

Who's afraid?

Just in case you ask what happened next?
It's the same, every time. She tells him
her anger at what he said, he lets out
a little of his, some right, some wrong,
some crazy, same old, until after too long
the man she wanted to strangle has his
arms around her, and they are exhausted,
her head against his chest, his usual
calm pulse beating faster with the pain
they just put each other through,
the almost realising what they would do
if they went too far.
As if the love they are sure of after
cancels out the gunshots to their hearts.

Some things wanted

To go upstairs right now, find you
in the spare bed, lift
your body up lightly
and blow love along,
remind us both
how fragile things are, how soon
we could disappear, how stupidly
we weigh ourselves down with tin cans
full of junk, just the props
of some spaghetti western where
nobody is very good with guns,
when all we really wanted to do
was let loose the horses, lie in the sun.
To kiss you and say sorry.

Scattered atoms

It's all about entropy:
how everything in creation moves
from organised
to purposeless bits –
fancy castles becoming piles of sand.

Our love,
how does it fit with this law? My loving
your hazel eyelashes,
big smooth finger-nails,
casual left arm-swing whilst walking –

could time pick up this love,
spread it like dust in the sunlight

so it's everywhere,
mixed with the busker's guitar-tunes in
Camden Town Underground,
the determined brush-strokes of Van Gogh?

Each ingredient: our kiss, that barking dog,
your searching hard for a line you lost –
one day all just a cocktail of murmurs
in an undifferentiated sky?

    And if so, will you
draw me nearer,
draw me until the light of us,
strewn around a diluted universe
is pulled back together, collides?

5-D

When time and space are folded
into an inkling of what is possible –
so tiny all could disappear,
so vast all boundaries lose meaning –
to escape limitation,
all that matters is a fifth dimension
which we touch upon
when we look at someone
we can call beloved.

Solved

I love you, she says.
I know, he replies.
She looks at his face,
the way his cheeks are creased
in a grin like a schoolboy
who came first at woodwork,
and all her study of meaning
is crystallised in a breath:
her heart knows what the brain
strives towards but may never touch –
love which is the physics of God.

In the holding

in the holding of the gift ... of communication

Shapes in clay
'Nel mezzo del cammin di nostra vita'
                ~ Dante Alighieri, *'The Divine Comedy'*

Do we take the seven letters of *'journey'*
and translate from them a meaning, just as Binyon did
Dante's *Commedia*?

Cammin meant 'journey' to him, 'story' to Carson,
'path' to James – all correlations drawing the reader
into an exchange.

Do we use every moulding of letters – be it English or Italian –
as a shape for our responses to fill
with flashes triggered by the brain's columns of experience?

Like countless piles of coins,
each one a different colour or height,
and when we choose a pile, the coins pay for a display.

So, I read *journey*, see hydrangea bushes, feel disco kisses,
sense tumour cells, fear – each of these words again
meaning something different to me than you.

How beautiful.

Lily

I held you, and in your lips saw centuries,
wisdom from your spirit home.
Your fingers showed me awe.
I held you, solid as a stone,
no confusion, needless fuss,
and the silence you put in my arms,
laid the kiss of angels on us.

C.

I turn into a stalker –
send her a poem called *'Shuddered'*
about the first time I read her book,
wear dark shades and stand under a yew,
drop cigarette butts at its roots,
rush up to tell her how great she was with that line
about old men welding; how she pumps blood
where I stay pale, then go –
pausing at the door to stare again at the girl
who seems to want to window-wipe the world.

Near Liboreiro

The old man on the steps of his house
by the water tap
each night calls out,
beats himself
for the death of his wife,
misses her so much,
and the guilt of it –
that she left before him
    or, who are we to say? –

is only made bearable by continuous
    slap, slap, slapping
of his own sides
    and chest:
certain he can never get them clean.

Years later he is still there,
inside me,
beating out a guilt

and I still want to hold him tight,
put my lips against his white hair
and kiss away

all that will not leave us,
all that we have no name for
but is inside,

dirty and hungry.

Oxford, night-swimming

Even now, too many attempts later,
there is the sound of perfect voices
and the clinking of blue glasses,
a slim girl with long hair taking off
bottle-green cords; a lot of smoke.

People stand around a small hidden reservoir
in the dark. We try to join in,
try to laugh the way they do,
say *My God!* and be cool – to dive in
naked and not go under.

Why Salmon Jump
(on discovering Raymond Carver, August 1989)

I sit cross-legged on the floor with Beata, my Polish friend.
There's a painting of a fish on the wall,

golden-yellow light, blue walls,
but mostly it's twenty minutes of an ordinary day.

We pass the book one to the other.
She reads me some lines.

I say *Yes*, she is right, and we read on.
To each other. Quickly. Silently. To each other again.

Sipping and gulping and swallowing
as though we've found new water.

No Translation
(for a boy called James)

1984.
We were volunteering as two school-girls
on a lock-up ward for the 'mentally handicapped'.
There were teeth marks on the window-sills.
Nurse told a woman who was leaning
on my shoulder, not to bite.

James was the only 'mental'
person we saw, who did not look it.
Not even once we knew.

Not in his face, his eyes, his stance.
He was clearly beautiful.
Had blond hair. Waves.

His 3-walled compartment was full of posters:
I said *Look! Ziggy Stardust!*
I've got him on my wall at home.

Then nurse told us about the car-crash
and somehow 'brain-damaged' made things easier.
Like a slot almost found.

But still the out-of-kilter disturbed.
We looked at each other, found no translation
for someone like this:

put aside, outside our world,
but who we could fall in love with.

if 'red' were 'God'

The poetry is so good I know it's one of those magazines I will want to read over; full of new words like 'asininity' and images intense, obscure, true. But half-way through I see again a colour missing. A woven blanket without any red. Not only that but where red is gone there is nothing strong enough to replace it, just a baby-peach like my nana used for doll bonnets: almost ugly, it is so lacking.

I stand up to hold the blanket to the air and a cold wind blows through the weak peachy holes, with no resistance. I think of times when it would not be conceivable to separate the red out of everyday life, would be like saying don't ever say the word *yes* today; don't even nod your head…

the sound of quietness

I

it is the snow along the hand-rail of the bridge
as I push a woollen glove along the rail and
blocks fall off into the river –
the barely detectable sound of
clumps falling onto water then
disappearing into liquid;
the tread of boots
across the bridge, over
the stile and onto the hillside, all the while
still knowing that slide of a hand along
the bridge-rail, pushing snow off
in long chunks, odd
bits dissolving
even as they touch a warm glove.

II

it is the elderly couple who lived
across the road with an only child
who hardly spoke, the bonfire night
when there was treacle-toffee on a plate
in their kitchen and three rockets
in milk bottles in their back yard, the father
moving about to set them off, the young girl
taking toffee in her hand, waiting
for the rockets to explode, like the quiet stars
would for one night, riot –
but now the fireworks make barely a sound,
they *pooof* and lights flash in the night sky
but quickly fade into darkness, dissolve silently into it
soft as snow bits hitting the river.

Who can tell?

Now then, who can tell me what this one's about?
he says. *In fact,* he continues, getting a gleam to his eyes,
I'll give this orange to anyone who can tell me.
We all glance at the fruit by the note-pad in front of him.
In fact, he goes on, now becoming so chuffed he could
conduct a song about it,
*I'll give TWO oranges to anyone who can prove me wrong
about the meaning of this poem!*

And he grapples in his rucksack on the floor
to pull out another juicy fruit,
puts it proudly next to the other, then looks at us.

We all offer answers like miscarriage; the loss of a young child.
No! No! he declares, thrilled like he's found the formula
to some cryptic combination lock.
Abortion! he says. *It's about an abortion!*

And all the class nod and go *oh yeah, oh yeah,
we see it now.* And I join in, despite myself.

Some words are mine

Like the 'down'
in C. K. Williams' first horse going down
or 'brain tumour', 'Blencathra', 'Scotland'.
They are my own.
I hear them –
reach out to possess,
pull them back:
words
so big,
without them
my feet would stumble.

Track through

      Nouns like *bitterness, jealousy, disdain,*
for me dissect their emotions to create a taste of them –
a memory almost physical –
      while *glee, wonder, awe* fail in any kind of capture,
take me only to a fence with no ladder to climb,
      no clear recounting of when I once made it over.

Why does no word exactly pin down the feeling
when we clear a ditch which we thought
might defeat us,
      or kiss after days of not speaking,
get out of the car to look at miles of purple heather?

Because are we looking for a prize we are afraid to name
in case the track through the haze to find it
is then closed?

Do we find an easy route between emotions which reduce us
      and their words,
because such feelings do belong within human limitation,
      while those which expand us are playing with containment
like a wild horse who knows the gate to the ring is open

      and gallops around us, for the joy of it?

In the holding

in the holding of the gift ... of mortal, human life

Can we fail?

When you give him all the love you have
but he still quits rehab and steals for the next fix,

when you fight and pray and fight to eliminate
every single monster cell, but you lose your fight,

when at your daughter's wedding you're so choked up
you drink too much and try to kiss the vicar,

when you need to stop before the summit, make the best
of a damned fine view, while others carry on,

when you know they want you to say yes to another operation
but really you want to say no, I'm ready to go,

you still don't fail. In the holding of the gift we turn it around
in the morning light and, for a few moments, succeed.

For Derek, who is blind
'You must go on. I can't go on. I'll go on'
~ Samuel Beckett, 'The Unnameable'

I pass you sat on a bench with your dog.
I'm in a rush but can't help saying *hi* and we get talking.

We talk about the weather and how's business.
I tell you about my visit soon to Iona. You reply
that several times you've considered the same –
going to a place for quiet contemplation.

But really we aren't talking about any of this, not much.
We are sat together on a bench while Bonnie sits at your feet,
her harness to the ground, and in the sharing of words
we salute each other.

I am strengthened by your courage to get up each morning
and make your way through town – always smart, always
a warm *hello*. Once, when you suggested you'd had enough,

it shook my own courage for days.
Whatever, we pass ten minutes, and continue.

Phuc
(for Phuc, who grew up in Hoi An Orphanage, Vietnam)

You are with me tonight because you did not stand out.
You were not the cutest child or one left to fade under a blanket.

When the staff served food or hosed children down,
you were not the most cruelly treated or one washed more gently.

When we finally got permission to take you all to the beach,
you were not someone I held, sat next to or laughed with.

You were just there, trying to get a look in, trying to be noticed.
I know I did because I am writing about you here.

The boy whose name is a little awkward for the tourists; who
couldn't fail to have a go.

A young man now, at the Adult Shelter, still with your
ability to survive, not with great flair but with persistence.

I think of lanterns kept in corners, sandcastles refusing to be
flattened – but prefer just the image of you.

Phuc was one of the children who inspired us to set up The Kianh Foundation for children with disabilities in central Vietnam (www.kianh.org.uk).

At ease

As we wait for the session to begin
I notice your bright tartan mini-dress,
spangled tights, blue beads.
The yoga teacher comes to stand
in front of you… isn't sure what
to say…*You can't wear that…*
is the gist of it…*But I will*…is your reply…
Just been out for lunch, your fabulous clincher.
I spend the rest of the afternoon
noting how elegant is your back arch,
your inverted pose, your 'dancer'–
watch you hitch up your skirt and not care.

Most of all feeling a little taste of love
for the freedom you put in the air.

Some vile tornado

I go visit him on the ward
and the canny old man I knew
to have a chat with in town, who
came in our shop to buy
lovely big Valentines
has all but gone
as if
some vile tornado has
sucked him
almost empty –
but he will not let go, he
holds
onto the bed-rails,
won't be taken until they bring his wife –
three days he remains till
they collect her from another ward
to be by his bedside to
say goodbye –
until then he
will not extinguish but
clings to life
with the force of his love
defying the whorl of death,
which is becoming
furious.

18th Birthday at Bolton Street Working Men's Club

Wendy Brown has turned up so we can dance Adam-Ant-style,
kicking our legs to each side, looking wild,
and I've got a man I'm sure I love
watching me from the bar,
and we're high on a belief,
a young untested faith
that life will carry on this good,
because it does;

we're sweet on an absence of what comes after this,
absence of a taste like paint in the throat
that right now
can't even be thought about,
is so far from being imagined
it's almost a joke.

Tinfoil and curls

They sit drinking coffee and he tells her
how, as a medical student, he had
observed her operation, did only
small assistance things but had been there
when the surgeon sawed open her head,
cut into her brain.

She feels funny when he tells her –
secretly witnessed, exposed;
even jealous that he had seen things while
she was out cold;
seen inside.

But she wants to hold him tight when he describes
how the surgeon had protected her hair
from being shaved off –
had wrapped
every
ringlet of curls
in tinfoil –
slow,
careful,
to keep them
away from harm.

1st Choice

1st choice would be a shark.

To wait, knowing,
hold my breath hard –
hair swirling like a mermaid.

I'd begin to panic with second thoughts
I bet.
Drunk with adrenaline I'd thrash about –

at least not wasting it,
ending with morphine and
brain-numbed pallor.

As the shark approached
I would stare in its slit eye,
prepare to be chunked,

for the pain and blood gush,
sea going red
with bits of me –

at least not fading,
a cartwheeling spark becoming
a faint blubbering *pity me.*

As I am torn apart
I'd experience death at full velocity,
     even saturate, as I claw for life –

        at least feel close
        to something exquisite;
        sublime.

Uncovered

Someone who spent holidays in Wales
under mum's beach cape
or playing in caves,

who ached to lie out of the shade –
dreamed of bikini poses by a pool
under hot brilliant beams –

but almost never did.

    Now the skin has become a territory to patrol,
silver scales have been peeled
back and fallen –

wooosh! –

to the ground, leaving her exposed,
like a Pippa doll with all her clothes taken off
being paraded in front of the family.

but by loving

not because time may just turn up,
not because a mortal smack
has shaken every perspective –
      '*make the most of this moment,*
      you never know when…' –
not this, because the frailty
so scares me, no,
not by duelling death
but by taking permission
to play fool with time,
to say *you have no power now,*
you cannot step in,
you are not the currency most precious…

Show me a day
'Show me a day when the world wasn't new'
        ~ Sister Barbara Hance (1928-1993)

when blackberries don't taste like a stolen prize
taken from the hedgerow, for the first time,

when the goldfinch at the feeder doesn't amaze
with how many sunflower seeds he can swallow

and the cat doesn't look like she never found
such a delicious fire to warm her belly by.

Show me a day when you look up at the stars
as you walk to the front door after a hard night

and suddenly feel like a child, held in a blanket
easily forgotten, sequined with silver, safe as home,

when the wait for news is harder than the news itself
and you surprise yourself with how much you can bear.

How lucky you are, despite everything, to be here.

Oneness

In the old stable, on top of three long branches
        we had propped against a wall for future
firewood,
           two blackbirds have made their home –
in the cup where the three ends meet.

Weeks ago, I saw them putting twigs there
and now
        watch the mates fly in and out with worms –
think
      what if one branch moves and everything collapses?

But the birds fly in and out,
        in and out, singing, flying,
and above them, above the blackbirds
in their precarious nest, are swallows in the rafters,
              whizzing out over me
here on the bench
and
      swooping
              from high –

no time for anything but flight,
      insects,

and I lean back as all boundaries disappear,
as I breathe out blackbirds,
      breathe in sky.

Clear

She comes upon the word 'exposed'.
That's it, nearly.
Something the mind rotates until the heart is raw –
the refusal to squeeze through a gap
into open blue.
    After so long carrying it about,
this imposed slaughter,
it begins to clear away now,
like a scowl drawn on window-water.

pondering on why did God make us?...

or was it…

at first just…

or is it this –

One great elephant who wants to create a lake
so She can see Her reflection in it,

and then She creates a breeze,
to ruffle the water…?

Something good to think about

In many different places,
like looking at a single buttercup in a meadow of buttercups,
or a grey stone in a river, spider on the wall,
to think, what if that is actually God, incognito?
God compressed into a single spider or stone,
directing the whole universe from
one spot, enjoying the fact nobody knows,
and then to think –
but then again that *is* God, because –
then lose the thread and
just stare at the buttercup or the
stone or the whatever, and
look around us,
be happy enough.

Jerusalem
(for my grandad, who was a Methodist preacher)

I put the cross in your hand,
closed your palm around it,
squeezed twice,
tried to hope you could understand.
I told you over again where it was from,
Jerusalem,
wanted you to see how special it was,
how much I loved you,
      but it was a light plastic cross
and your mind was heavy with dying.

So, I tried to remember you
speaking in a high funny voice to your poodle,
Princess Tina, meeting you out of the factory
in your overalls, smelling of flour,
walking with you around Stanley football field,
excited it was just us, together,
and the one time I saw you preach –
we sang 'Lord of the Dance'.

Then, I looked at you and whispered to my nan,
from my heart to her place in heaven,
to please look over you, send God to you,
and would He take you, gently, very soon.

But He didn't. It was not gentle.
If God called you home, it was a call I do not understand.
How lucky we are that faith
goes deeper than reason, deeper than belief.

It's not the same

We can turn around fear to hope to grief to joy,
all in a burning forest

but faith stands alone,
the tall stone that reaches above the smoke,

does not exchange itself
or find relief in cindered leaves.

Faith is to feel, when all other feelings have given up
or fled,
and with each breath know you are safe.

Bravery

Pure light. Not known by exposure to darkness.
Constant health, joy, hope.
Could bravery – through love –
to step into this,
be all we are missing, in this life?

On the same street as the posh shoe-shops

The door is just about open:
crammed wooden hangers spewing clothes out
in a banquet of colours:
pea-green cotton blouse cuff,
turquoise shirt collar, blood-red velvet,
and that gorgeous yellow jumper.

But *I'm not really open,* the lady mutters.
She pushes the mop of white hair
away from her face
and looks contentedly-exasperated.
Not really open, not really closed
she seems to be saying
as the reluctant-to-give-up
hustle past her doorstep.

People push against each other
in the pleasure of it all,
the irregularity,
on such a perfect street as this –
as if the dim light inside
is a peaty vapour to be breathed,
a defiance of progress-proper
we all want to be drenched in…

As we paw through the deep pile of clothes
on the floor – thick corduroy coats,
old tweeds – it's as if we could keep going and come out
somewhere else,
no longer caring why we are in this city –
or even whether anything

outside of this room
really exists.

Identity

I

Not being a mum

I stand in the school yard waiting for Jess. His dad has asked me to bring him home which is only about 200 yards but is enough. I stand looking at all the mums and grandparents and think *this is what it's like;* lean on the wall and try to keep still, not stare at people's coats. I enjoy thinking how recently I took Jess to the park and we had a great time at the swings; how he trusted me to push him quite high, held my hand at the climbing frame. My heart gets a bit giddy as time for the kids to come out approaches. I start panicking he'll not recognise me or want to walk towards me and then, two minutes to go, his dad arrives saying he had time to come, after all. I say *fine* and walk back with them then head into town; like I've been spotted.

II

Call her Marchioness

She was a loan pony, not one of ours, so I didn't know her well like the others. Her name I forget. All I know is that one day she would not cross a ditch in the back forest. A small muddy ditch which she refused to tread or jump, so the whole twenty-long trek was held up. We all had a go, all the horse-girls, ended up bringing the boss over from the farm – our own Marlon Brando, trying to force or persuade with whip, boot, talk, until eventually he said *let her go, she deserves it. She'll make her own way back.* So we did, we turned her loose, returned to base without her. I still respect her for it. Think of her thick knotted mane and, on our way back to the farm, my horse's ears, twitching.

Can Tell

I watch you through the window,
walking back from the Post Office, towards our shop.
Can tell it's you even from far off, the way you swing
your left arm with each step, swing it
with a slight cheerfulness across your chest
like some boy from the bakery
going fishing after work, a lad on return
from posting a note to his girl.

As you come closer I catch the slight glow to your face –
a ruddy innocence.
How you hold your smile in a quite specific way;
it says *I am a quiet man, let me pass.*
I hear your footsteps to a distinct beat,
see the tufts to your hay-time hair,
the worn shiny patches on your cords,

and I'm the swallow flying in
after a hard journey north.

Last winter

You tell me how peculiar it is to see them resting so high in a tree.
They slept there over-night, the five of them.
Big blue beautiful bodies perched in the top branches.
You point as we stare at the marvel of their blueness
against the brown winter twigs.
I never knew they went so high! you say,
both of us on the hotel drive, taking them in,
me admiring them because you do –
and in the beholding, we feel something
weave through me, you, the peacocks, the trees.

Laid flat on the mesh-metal bridge

She lies with arms out wide,
above her a ring of silver-birch tree-tops,
the sun back-lighting their gold,

    and in the centre a blue autumn sky,
      strips of cirrus cloud,
    in the foreground a moth.

She thinks *nothing could be
more than this,*
and knows it to be true

in a way that clears her cells,
takes away
all the clutter.

She falls asleep
to the river underneath her
then wakes and the light is gone

and it is not
the most beautiful sight,
is more dull, cold,

but she knows what she has seen,
and that changes the truth of everything.

Permanence

What if our haste to taste every drop
(or run and hide), is not after all in fear of mortality,

of the clock being wound finite times,
but of our immortality, the *forever* inside us?

What if the panic deep in our cells which makes us
shout out at our brother for having no answers

is really a panic our fire never goes out,
that within us is a spark so full of force it could

bounce off car bonnets and explode windows,
a light so bright it could vapourize an ocean?

What if the fear in almost every person on earth
is not of their dying but of their being born

to a life so full of potential to grow it is thought safer
to stay enclosed, in suits of armour which we call injuries?

or in the arm-link of a friend
(on Iona)

I don't find you on Port Ban beach today, in the warm
                         glittering stones,
or up on Dun I in the heavy rain where wild geese stand motionless
        then take off suddenly in a flamboyant clamour.
I don't find you there.

Or yesterday in the chapel when I was sitting quiet until
                         chattering tourists
came in taking photographs, but then sat silent
behind me, deep in prayer, and I scolded my too fast judgement.

Not in waiting at the pier for my loved one to make it
on the last ferry before the gales set in,
tears when I couldn't see him,
                embarrassed joy
when he came waving, and the fishermen laughed.

I don't find you, which is an honest thing,
when I am awkward to be so sure,
but finding you isn't what my heart does,
because you, God, are here.

Purple

November, and spent dock is heading
back to the ground,

bird-cherry trees
have lost their bundled cities of caterpillar moths

while
willow leaves attempt a final tango by the pond.

But no-one told this purple flower.
The news of time was muddled in her bud

and out she came, amongst decaying
thistles on her street,

half-way up a line
of forlorn and long-closed doors,

this keen new thing,
eager for sunshine and trumpets,

calling for bees to plunge
into her cushion of hope,

and all of life by the riverside
is lifted from sleep.

Jo and Bess

You say you don't like marmalade
so I say it's just orange jam,

you don't like big trees
so I say they're corrals for leaves,

you think squirrels are scary,
so I say they're ponies for elves.

You say you suddenly can't spell *heaven*
so I say try *heave* (as in pull)
with an 'n' on.

You say being in this place feels weird,
so I say imagine sitting by the Mississippi
on a big log.

You say why does it all come back
the same, every day,
the same world out there, in here?

I say let's close our eyes, and behind them
it can all be a perfect somewhere,

you in your cowboy clothes,
two fine grey mares standing by

while we make coffee on a campfire.
You say you don't want to close your eyes,

    so I close mine, tell you of galloping horses.

Indigo Dreams Publishing Ltd
24, Forest Houses
Cookworthy Moor
Halwill
Beaworthy
Devon
EX21 5UU
www.indigodreams.co.uk